Enter the legendary arena of rugby with "The 50 legends of rugby an[...]   [...]ook transports you into t[...]   [...]ne of the most exciting and [...]   [...]time. From moments of gl[...]   [...]very page of this collection is infused with the spirit of camaraderie, courage and determination that characterizes this iconic sport.

Prepare to experience an unforgettable adventure alongside the heroes of rugby, legends who have marked the history of this sport with their performances on the field and their impact on global sporting culture. From Jonah Lomu to Jonny Wilkinson, each player has written his own epic, shaping rugby into a true spectacle of strength, speed and strategy.

This book is much more than a simple collection of sporting exploits, it invites you to discover behind the scenes of the locker rooms, the intense rivalries and the emotional moments shared with supporters around the world. Immerse yourself in captivating stories, relive legendary matches and feel the electrifying atmosphere of stadiums where rugby history has been written.

SUMMARY

#1- JONAH LOMU

#2- RICHIE MCCAW

#3- DAN CARTER

#4- BRIAN O'DRISCOLL

#5- GARETH EDWARDS

#6- JONNY WILKINSON

#7- SERGE BLANCO

#8- MARTIN JOHNSON

#9- FRANÇOIS PIENAAR

#10- JEAN-PIERRE RIVES

#11- DAVID CAMPESE

#12- JOHN EALES

#13- COLIN MEADS

#14- SEAN FITZPATRICK

#15- PHIL BENNETT

#16- JPR WILLIAMS

#17- WAISALE SEREVI

#18- MICHAEL JONES

#19- TIM HORAN

#20- GEORGE GREGAN

#21- MARK ELLA

#22- THIERRY DUSAUTOIR

#23- VICTOR MATFIELD

#24- OS DU RANDT

#25- NELSON MANDELA*

SUMMARY

JONAH LOMU

BORN MAY 12, 1975 IN AUCKLAND, NEW ZEALAND

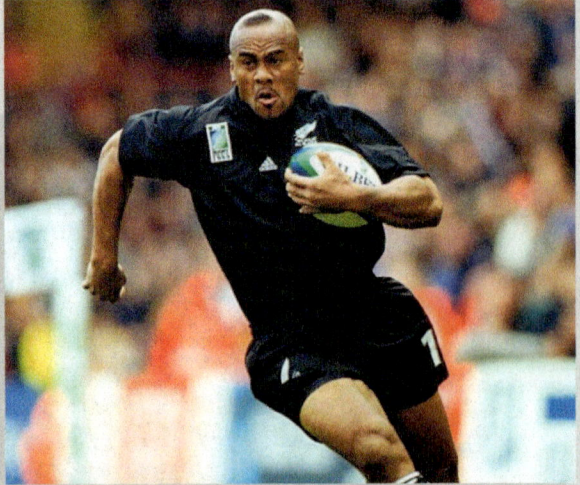

Jonah Lomu has left an indelible mark on the world of rugby. Although he never won the Rugby World Cup, his impact on the field was monumental. He appeared in 63 matches for the All Blacks, scoring 37 tries. He played for several clubs in New Zealand and overseas, contributing greatly to their success.

THE PHENOMENON THAT REVOLUTIONIZED RUGBY

Jonah Lomu has redefined the role of the winger in modern rugby. His unique blend of height (1.96 m), weight (approximately 119 kg), and speed was unprecedented, making him an unstoppable force on the field. His performances at the 1995 Rugby World Cup, where he scored seven tries, propelled him onto the international stage. His devastating runs, his ability to break down defenses and his surprising speed make him an exceptional and unforgettable player.

One of the highlights of his career was his incredible performance at the 1995 World Cup, particularly his try against England in the semi-final, where he literally crushed defenders in his path. Off the field, his fight against a rare kidney disease and his resilience in the face of health challenges have inspired millions. His legacy extends beyond rugby; he became a symbol of determination and courage, influencing an entire generation of players and fans. Jonah also played an important role in promoting rugby internationally and establishing New Zealand as a sporting superpower.

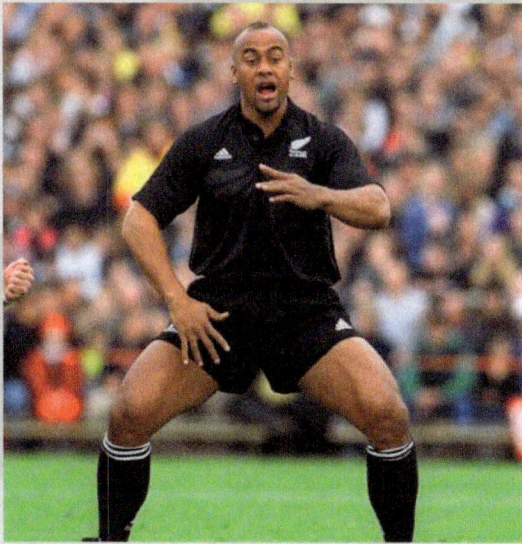

After receiving a kidney transplant in 2003, he made a brief return to competition in 2005, at the highest club level with the Welsh Cardiff Blues, before stopping in 2007

RICHIE MCCAW
"CAPTAIN FANTASTIC"

BORN DECEMBER 31, 1980 IN OAMARU, NEW ZEALAND

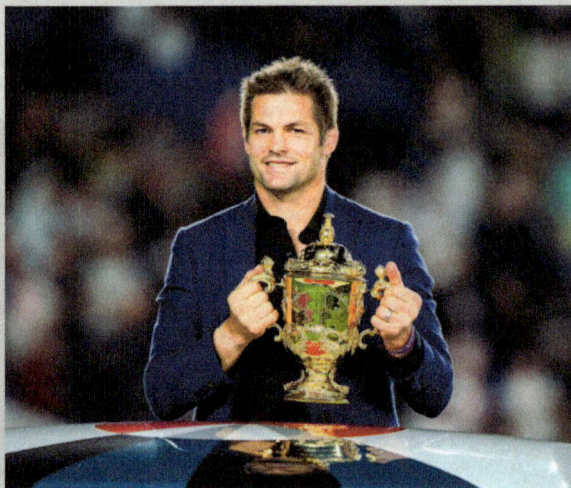

Richie McCaw is arguably one of the most decorated rugby players in history. Iconic captain of the All Blacks, he won the Rugby World Cup twice, in 2011 and 2015. He holds the world record for the number of test matches played (148) and was named World Rugby Player of the Year three times. times.

THE LORD OF THE RUCKS AND THE STEADFAST CAPTAIN

Richie McCaw is famous for his incredible longevity, resilience and steadfast leadership. His playing intelligence, his impeccable technique as a flanker, and his ability to always be in the right place at the right time set him apart. His remarkable performances, his consistency at the highest level and his ability to inspire and motivate his teammates are legendary. McCaw is not only a great player, but a true ambassador for rugby.

Richie McCaw left an indelible mark on rugby. He led the All Blacks to an impressive series of victories, demonstrating unwavering skill and determination. His approach to the game, characterized by his tenacity and fair play, was exemplary. He was at the heart of memorable moments, such as the triumph at the 2011 and 2015 World Cups, solidifying his place among the greats. His leadership on and off the field positively influenced his teammates and opponents, making him a role model for future generations.

McCaw once paraglided with a New Zealand flag attached to his harness to celebrate a victory.

DAN CARTER, "DC"

BORN MARCH 5 1982 IN LEESTON, NEW ZEALAND

His record is as rich as it is impressive, including two Rugby World Cup victories (2011 and 2015) with the All Blacks. Dan Carter was named World Rugby Player of the Year in 2005, 2012 and 2015, and holds the record for most points scored in international tests.

OPENING MASTERY AND KICKING GENIUS

Dan Carter is famous for his incredible talent, precision with his feet, and strategic skill. He symbolizes elegance and precision in rugby, capable of changing the course of a match with his surgical passes, strategic runs and decisive kicks. His scoring record, calmness under pressure, and ability to lead his team to victory in critical moments established Carter as a model of consistency and excellence.

Carter made rugby history with his legendary performances. His triumphant return at the 2015 World Cup, after a disappointment in 2011 due to injury, is an illustration of his determination and commitment to the sport. At club level, he was a major contributor to the Crusaders' success and brought his expertise and leadership to European teams. His ability to positively influence his teammates, his commitment to the game, and his dedication to excellence make him a respected and admired ambassador for rugby.

On June 12, 2010, he was the fourth scorer to pass 1,000 points scored for the national team, after the All Blacks' victory against Ireland 66–28 in a test match.

BRIAN O'DRISCOLL,"BOD"

BORN JANUARY 21 1979 IN DUBLIN, IRELAND

With an international career spanning from 1999 to 2014, he captained the Irish national team and the British and Irish Lions. Brian O'Driscoll won four Triple Crowns with Ireland and is the third most capped player in the world with 141 test matches. He also won the Six Nations Grand Slam in 2009.

THE MAGICIAN OF THE CENTER AND THE INSPIRING CAPTAIN

Brian O'Driscoll is famous for his leadership, his longevity and his ability to change the course of matches thanks to his game intelligence. His solid defense, his dynamic breakthroughs and his ability to make decisive interceptions have often turned perilous situations around. His impact extends beyond Ireland's borders, making him a respected figure around the world. His records, including the most tries in the Six Nations, are testament to his exceptional talent.

The most notable moments of his career include his spectacular performances at the Six Nations and World Cups, as well as his heroic appearances on the British and Irish Lions tours. His try against Australia in 2001 during his first tour with the Lions remains an iconic moment. His longevity, his dedication to his sport and his ability to inspire both his teammates and his opponents make him a legend. Even after his retirement, his influence continued through his work as a commentator and analyst, contributing to the growth and popularity of rugby.

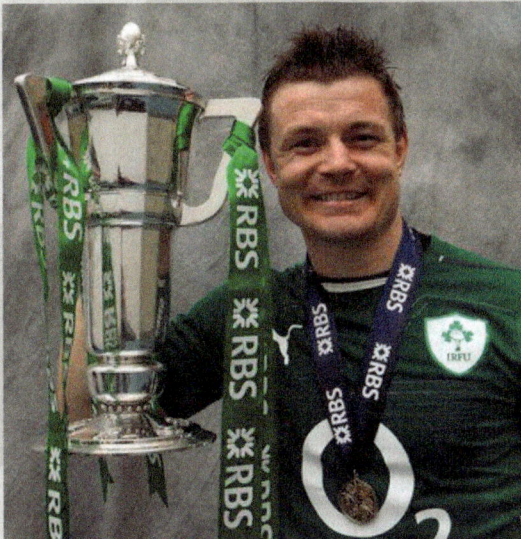

In 2015, during the World Rugby awards, Brian O'Driscoll received with the Australian Nathan Sharpe the merit award awarded by the IRPA (International Rugby Players Association)

GARETH EDWARDS "THE KING"

Gareth Edwards played for Wales and the British & Irish Lions. He won three Grand Slams with Wales in the Five Nations Tournament and was a key part of the Lions' invincible tours of 1971 to New Zealand and 1974 to South Africa.

THE MAESTRO OF THE MELEE AND THE GENIUS OF THE GAME

Gareth Edwards is famous for his vision, speed, agility and instinct, which made him a rugby legend. He was renowned for his ability to control the game, make precise passes and make quick decisions under pressure. His try for the Barbarians against the All Blacks in 1973 is often cited as the greatest try of all time, perfectly illustrating his creativity and genius on the field.

Gareth Edwards' career is punctuated by memorable moments that have not only defined his own achievements, but also contributed to the history of rugby. His performances for Wales and the British and Irish Lions are legendary. His leadership, work ethic and competitiveness have made him a role model for future generations. He is widely credited with elevating the scrumhalf role to an artistic level, influencing the way the position is played to this day.

In 1997, Gareth Edwards was one of the fifteen greatest international rugby union players of the past inducted into the International Rugby Hall of Fame.

JONNY WILKINSON, "WILKO"

BORN MAY 25, 1979 IN FRIMLEY, ENGLAND

His track record includes England's iconic 2003 Rugby World Cup victory, where he scored the decisive drop goal in the final against Australia. He also won several English Championship titles with Newcastle Falcons and had Top 14 success with Toulon, winning back-to-back European Cup titles.

THE DROP MAESTRO AND WORLD CUP HERO

Jonny Wilkinson is famous for his incredible footing precision, iron discipline, and unrivaled work ethic. His drop goal in the 2003 World Cup final has become an iconic moment in rugby history, a symbol of determination and precision under pressure. His ability to score from any angle and distance, combined with his tenacious defense and leadership on the court, made him a respected and feared player.

Wilkinson's career has been marked by success and remarkable performances. His precision, calm under pressure and total commitment to his sport have made him indispensable to England and its clubs. Despite recurring injuries, his resilience and determination to return to the highest level inspired many players and fans. At club and national level, his contribution to the game and his ability to positively influence the outcome of matches are undisputed. His retirement in 2014 marked the end of an era, but his legacy lives on through future generations of players.

In December 2002, Jonny Wlkinson was awarded an MBE, First Degree of the Order of the British Empire.

SERGE BLANCO, "EL BLANCO"

BORN AUGUST 31, 1958 IN CARACAS, VENEZUELA

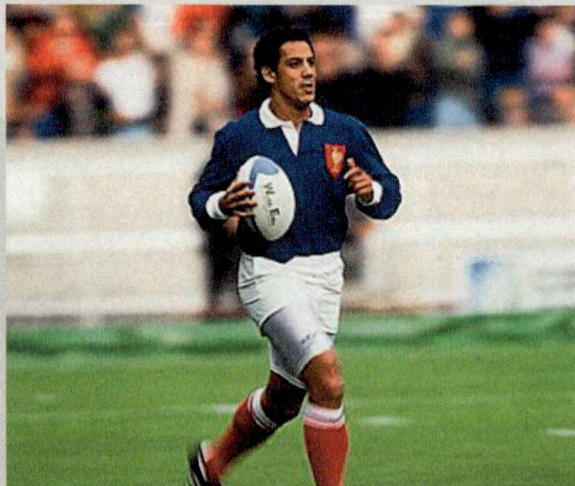

His record includes 93 caps for the French team between 1980 and 1991, with which he won five Five Nations Tournaments, including two Grand Slams. Serge Blanco also scored 38 tries, a record for France at the time of his retirement. Blanco is famous for his flamboyant style of play, his elegance on the pitch.

THE RUGBY ARTIST AND THE MAGICIAN OF THE BACKS

Serge Blanco is famous for his elegant style of play, his flair, and his ability to make spectacular runs from the back. His speed, agility, and sense of the game have made him a formidable opponent. His decisive try against Australia in the semi-final of the 1987 World Cup remains one of the most emblematic moments of his career and of French rugby, perfectly illustrating his ability to change the course of a match.

Beyond his exploits on the field, Serge Blanco left his mark on rugby with his charisma and leadership. He was a pioneer for French rugby, raising the level of the game and inspiring many generations of players. After his career he was also involved in rugby administration, contributing to the management and development of the sport. His commitment to rugby and his legacy as an exceptional player continue to inspire respect and admiration.

Blanco played his entire career at Biarritz Olympique.

MARTIN JOHNSON, "JOHNNO"

BORN MARCH 9, 1970 IN SOLIHULL, ENGLAND

Martin Johnson is one of the most accomplished players in English rugby. He captained the England team that won the Rugby World Cup in 2003. He also led Leicester Tigers to several Premiership titles and won two European Cups with the club.

THE RUGBY GIANT AND THE STEADFAST CAPTAIN

Martin Johnson is famous for his exceptional leadership, imposing physical strength and intimidating presence on the field. He spearheaded the England team, leading to major victories with undisputed authority. His ability to inspire and motivate his teammates was crucial in winning the 2003 World Cup.

The greatest moment of his career undoubtedly remains the victory in the World Cup in 2003, where his leadership was a determining factor. His performances for club and country have set new standards of achievement and excellence. His successful transition as coach and manager of the England team demonstrates his continued commitment to rugby. His approach to the game, characterized by unwavering determination and rigorous discipline, continues to influence players and coaches around the world.

Johnson announced his international retirement in January 2004 after long months of reflection since the end of the World Cup, he has a total of 84 caps, including 39 as captain.

FRANÇOIS PIENAAR

BORN JANUARY 2, 1967 IN VEREENIGING, SOUTH AFRICA

François Pienaar is known for having been the captain of the South African team which won the World Cup in 1995. The Springboks defeated New Zealand in the final, a match which became emblematic of the post-apartheid era in South Africa. Pienaar also had a successful club career with Transvaal, with whom he won several titles.

A CAPTAIN FOR UNITY

His leadership, his strength of character and his closeness to Nelson Mandela have become symbols of national unity and reconciliation in a country freshly emerged from apartheid. His ability to unite a diverse team and channel the potential of his players was essential to their success. The image of him receiving the World Cup from Nelson Mandela, both wearing the number 6 jersey, remains one of the most powerful in sport.

In addition to his World Cup victory, Pienaar is recognized for his significant contribution to South African rugby, both on and off the field. His leadership and commitment to the sport made him a respected figure and a role model for future generations. After his retirement he continued to be involved in rugby and other philanthropic initiatives, contributing to the advancement of sport and South African society.

He has been a member of the International Rugby Hall of Fame since 2005.

JEAN-PIERRE RIVES
"GOLDEN HELMET"

BORN DECEMBER 31, 1952 IN TOULOUSE, FRANCE

Jean-Pierre Rives captained the French team 34 times, a record at the time, and led his team to numerous successes in the Five Nations Tournament, including two Grand Slams in 1977 and 1981. His club career with Stade Toulousain and Racing Club de France was also successful.

INDOMITABLE ENERGY AND THE SYMBOL OF COMBAT

Jean-Pierre Rives is famous for his passionate style of play, determination and courage on the pitch. He was known for his unwavering fighting spirit and his ability to get up from every tackle. His small size for a third line did not prevent him from becoming one of the most feared and respected players. Rives is not just a rugby player; he is also an artist, recognized for his sculptures, illustrating his versatility and creativity.

Rives left a lasting legacy in rugby, not only for his athletic prowess but also for his spirit and character. His performances as captain of the French team, notably during the Grand Slam victories, inspired an entire nation. His commitment to rugby and his dedication to the sport make him an iconic figure, often cited as a source of inspiration for rugby players and fans of the sport.

After his rugby career, he became a recognized sculptor.

DAVID CAMPESE, "FIELD"

BORN OCTOBER 21, 1962 IN QUEANBEYAN, AUSTRALIA

David Campese won the 1991 World Cup with Australia and for a time held the record for most tries in international matches with 64 tries in 101 tests. His flamboyant play and exceptional talent have made him a legend of the sport, and he is often cited among the best players of all time.

THE MAGICIAN OF RUGBY

Campese is famous for his inventive style of play, characterized by evasive runs, daring feints and no-look passes. His ability to create the unexpected on the field has often confused his opponents and delighted the spectators. His "goose-step" technique (a deceptive movement to destabilize defenders) has become his trademark.

During his career, Campese had many memorable moments, including his performances at the 1991 Rugby World Cup, where his play was instrumental in Australia's victory. His daring challenges, his refusal to play conservatively and his always offensive spirit marked an era and influenced the playing style of subsequent generations. Off the field, his frank character and sometimes controversial statements have made him a respected media figure and commentator.

He becomes the second player in the world, after Frenchman Philippe Sella, to reach the number of hundred caps for the national team.

JOHN EALES, "NOBODY"

With the Australian national team, John Eales won two Rugby World Cups, in 1991 and 1999. He captained the Wallabies for several years, accumulating a total of 86 international caps and scoring 173 points, a remarkable record for a second line player.

THE GENTLEMAN OF RUGBY

John Eales is famous for his incredible versatility, leadership and sportsmanship. Capable of playing in the second or third line, he was also an accurate scorer, a rarity for a player in his position. His game was characterized by great intelligence, impeccable technique, and an ability to inspire and unite his team.

Among the defining moments of his career, his two World Cup victories and his role as an influential captain are particularly notable. Eales was also recognized for his outstanding club performances with the Queensland Reds in Super Rugby. His ability to make crucial throw-ins, score important points and guide his team in critical situations made him a central part of the Australian team for a decade.

He is one of Australia's most loved and respected sportsmen. Every year, he organizes the "John Eales Medal dinner" which rewards the best Australian rugby players of the year.

COLIN MEADS, "PINETREE"

BORN JUNE 3, 1936 IN CAMBRIDGE, NEW ZEALAND

Colin Meads is a legendary figure in New Zealand and world rugby. During his career he was capped 55 times for the All Blacks national team and played a total of 133 matches for New Zealand, a record at the time.

THE LEGEND OF THE ALL BLACK

Colin Meads is famous for his imposing physique, raw strength, and endurance. He was known for his ability to physically dominate opponents and inspire his teammates. Despite injuries and the rigors of the game, he rarely missed matches, showing exceptional resilience and tenacity. His presence on the field was so influential that his mere selection into the team was often enough to intimidate opponents.

Meads had many highlights, but his most memorable match might be against South Africa in 1970, where he played with a broken arm, showing incredible determination and toughness. His name remains synonymous with strength and determination in rugby, and he is often cited as one of the greatest players of all time. After his retirement, Meads continued to serve rugby as a coach, selector and administrator, contributing significantly to the sport he loved.

His brother Stanley was also an All Black between 1961 and 1966.

SEAN FITZPATRICK, "FITZY"

BORN JUNE 4, 1963 IN AUCKLAND, NEW ZEALAND

Sean Fitzpatrick was a central part of the All Blacks for most of his career, playing 92 international tests and leading the team as captain to numerous victories. He was part of the 1987 World Cup victory and was a constant mainstay of the team until his retirement in 1997.

THE ALL BLACKS WARRIOR

Fitzpatrick is famous for his tenacity, endurance and leadership on the field. He was known for his ability to lead the team in critical moments and for his fierce competitiveness. His ability to make precise throws and support the collective effort in the scrum has made him one of the best at his position.

His career is punctuated by many highlights, including the victorious 1987 World Cup campaign and his numerous victories as captain. His longevity and ability to maintain high level performance throughout his career is remarkable. After his retirement, Fitzpatrick continued to be an influential voice in the world of rugby, working as a commentator and participating in various initiatives to promote the sport.

Since May 2016, Sean Fitzpatrick has been Vice President and Academician of the Laureus Sport for Good Foundation.

PHIL BENNETT, "BENNY"

BORN OCTOBER 24, 1948 IN FELINFOEL, WALES

During his international career, Phil Bennett won several titles in the Five Nations Tournament, including two Grand Slams with Wales. He was also a key member of the British and Irish Lions, contributing to their historic winning streak in 1974.

THE WELSH DRAGON WIZARD

Phil Bennett is famous for his creative and daring style of play, marked by slalom runs, confusing feints and an ability to create openings where there seemed to be none. His technical skill and ability to read the game made him a formidable opponent. He is particularly memorable for his role in the British and Irish Lions' legendary victory in South Africa in 1974.

As well as his successes with Wales and the Lions, Bennett left a lasting legacy as an inspiration and innovator in rugby. His performances raised the standard of the Welsh game and influenced the way the fly half is played. He is often cited for his famous motivational speech before the match against England in 1977, which galvanized his team to a historic victory. His passion, commitment to excellence and love of the game continue to inspire players and fans.

In 2005, he entered the International Rugby Hall of Fame.

JOHN PETER RHYS WILLIAMS, "JPR"

BORN MARCH 2, 1949 IN BRIDGEND, WALES

JPR Williams was a mainstay of the Welsh team during the 1970s. He won several Five Nations Tournaments, including several Grand Slams. Williams was also a crucial member of the British and Irish Lions, particularly during the unbeaten tour of South Africa in 1974.

THE STEADFAST WELSH FULLBACK

JPR Williams is renowned for his courage, tenacity and exceptional defensive skills. His ability to make devastating tackles and his skill in counter-attacking from the back made him a feared opponent. Her long hair and distinctive headband have become iconic. Williams is also famous for his durability, having played at an international level for over a decade.

Among the most memorable moments of his career, his performances at the Welsh Grand Slams and his victorious participations on the Lions tours are particularly notable. He is particularly famous for his epic confrontations against the All Blacks, where his physical and determined play often prevailed. Following his retirement from international rugby, JPR Williams continued to make an impact on sport as an orthopedic surgeon, bringing his passion and commitment to the wellbeing and health of athletes.

JPR Williams is the eldest of four boys: his younger brothers are named Phil, Chris and Mike. Encouraged and coached by their father, the four boys spend most of their free time playing rugby union in the garden.

WAISALE SEREVI, "WATER"

BORN MAY 20, 1968 IN SUVA, FIJI

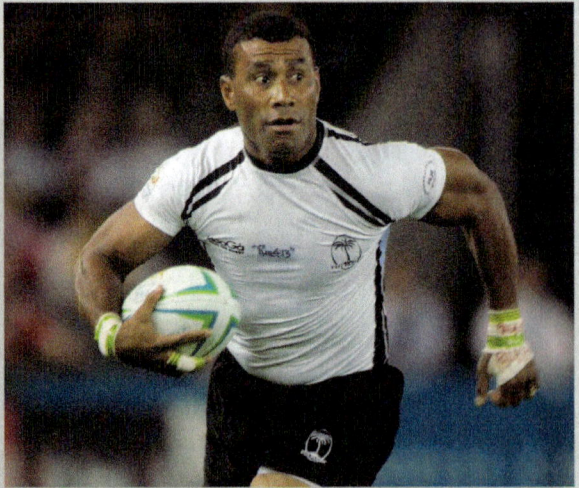

His record is dazzling, including several victories in the Hong Kong Sevens, considered the unofficial "world championships" of rugby sevens. Serevi also represented Fiji in rugby union, participating in the World Cup. However, it was in rugby sevens that his genius was fully expressed.

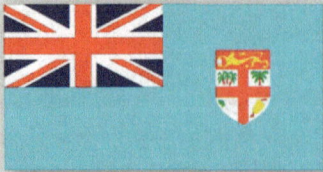

THE RUGBY VIRTUOSO IN SEPT

Serevi is famous for his ability to change the course of a match with a single move. His footwork, vision of the game and precise passing made him a feared opponent and a spectacle in his own right. He took rugby sevens to an artistic level, inspiring generations of players. His performances not only raised the profile of rugby sevens but also helped to showcase the talent and passion for rugby in Fiji.

Serevi played a crucial role in establishing Fiji as a rugby sevens superpower, winning numerous international tournaments and becoming an iconic figure in the sport. His innovative style of play and his ability to inspire his teammates were essential in these victories. Even after his retirement, Serevi continues to influence the sport as a coach, sharing his expertise and passion for rugby.

In fourteen years, Waisale Serevi played 38 matches with the Fiji team during which he scored eleven tries, forty conversions, twenty-seven penalties and three drops (221 points).

MICHAEL JONES, "THE ICEMAN"

BORN APRIL 8, 1965 IN AUCKLAND, NEW ZEALAND

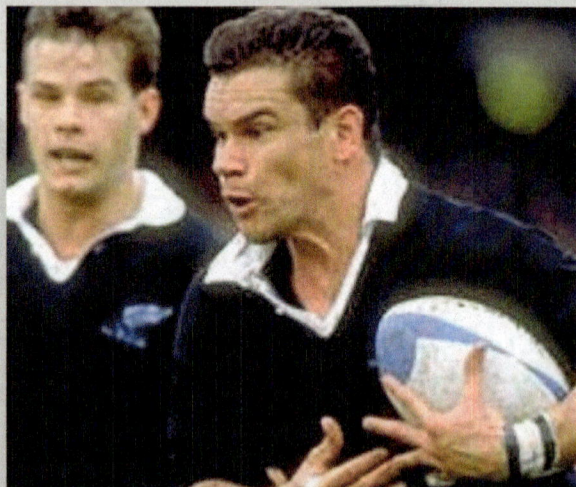

Michael Jones was a key part of the All Blacks for many years, playing in the 1987 World Cup and contributing to the team's victory. His international career is marked by exceptional performances which established him as a world-class player.

THE ETHICS AND ELEGANCE OF RUGBY

Michael Jones is famous for his incredible work ethic, dedication to the game and his ability to make devastating tackles as well as impactful runs. He was recognized for his incredible physical condition and his ability to read the game, anticipating and thwarting the opponent's moves. Jones was also one of the first to take on a modern flanker role, being a complete player, contributing in all aspects of the game.

One of Jones' most notable contributions was during the 1987 Rugby World Cup, where he was a mainstay of the All Blacks team that won the tournament. His career was also marked by his commitment to fair play and his decision not to play on Sundays due to his religious beliefs, which at times meant he missed crucial matches. Despite these absences, he remains a respected figure for his integrity and dedication to the sport.

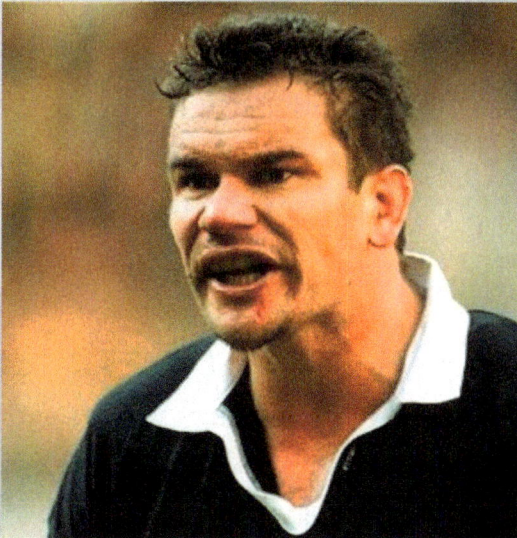

After being assistant coach of the Samoa team, he became its coach in 2004 and led it to the 2007 World Cup. He resigned after this competition, in which Samoa only finished fourth in their group, behind the Tongans. .

TIM HORAN
"HORAN THE HURRICANE"

BORN 18 MAY 1970 IN DARLINGHURST, SYDNEY, AUSTRALIA

His record includes two Rugby World Cup victories with Australia in 1991 and 1999, making him one of the few players to have won the Cup twice. Tim Horan also shone in Super Rugby with the Queensland Reds, showing exceptional skill in both attack and defence.

MASTER AU CENTER

Horan is famous for his vision of the game, his ability to create openings, and his defensive skills. His playing intelligence, speed and technical skills were second to none. He was a complete player, capable of making decisive tackles and breaking opposition lines with his hard-hitting runs. Horan was a fierce competitor, known for his ability to raise his game during important matches.

His return from injury for the 1999 World Cup after a serious knee injury and his key role in Australia's victory were particularly notable moments in his career. His ability to overcome adversity and perform at an exceptional level has inspired many players and fans. After his retirement, Horan continued to contribute to rugby as a commentator and analyst, sharing his expertise and passion for the game.

The 1999 title would mark the beginning of the twilight of his career. Often injured in 2000, he was left out of the national team then after a final season in Australia in 2000 with Brisbane South, he joined England to play for Saracens.

GEORGE GREGAN, "THE GENERAL"

BORN APRIL 19, 1973 IN LUSAKA, ZAMBIA

With 139 caps, George Gregan was the most capped player in a test match for Australia and long held the world record for caps. He was a key part of the Australian team that won the World Cup in 1999 and reached the final in 2003. Gregan also led the Brumbies to several Super Rugby successes.

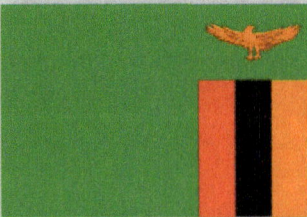

THE RUGBY STRATEGIST

George Gregan is famous for his playing intelligence, his passing accuracy and his ability to read and control the game. His tenacious defense and tactical management often frustrated opponents. He was known for his calm under pressure, resilience and inspiring leadership, often seen as the tactical mastermind behind his team's successes.

One of the most iconic moments of his career was his game-saving tackle on Jeff Wilson in 1994 against New Zealand. Gregan has also been a consistent model of professionalism and commitment, helping to raise the level of competition and performance in international rugby. After his retirement he remained involved in rugby and various charities, continuing to influence sport and society.

He ended his international career at the end of the quarter-final lost to England during the 2007 World Cup, starting 4 times in the 5 matches he played with Australia during the event.

MARK ELLA

BORN JUNE 5, 1959 IN LA PEROUSE, AUSTRALIA

Although his international career was relatively short, it was marked by some exceptional performances. Mark Ella played 25 Tests for Australia, captivating the world with his talent. Particularly memorable was his 1984 season, during which he scored a try in each of the Wallabies' four tests.

THE GAME ARCHITECT

Mark Ella is famous for his incredible sense of the game, his ability to create opportunities and his mastery of strategy on the pitch. His vision, his precise passes, and his ability to play under pressure made him a unique player. Ella was an innovative playmaker, often ahead of her time, with an approach to rugby that combined technique, intelligence and creativity.

His career, although short, was filled with memorable moments and left an indelible mark on rugby. He was an inspiration to many players and helped raise the profile of Australian rugby on the international stage. His decision to retire at the peak of his career, after a triumphant year in 1984, added to his myth and respect among fans and players.

To everyone's surprise, he ended his career following this tour, at the age of only 25, prioritizing his studies and being in conflict with coach Alan Jones.

THIERRY DUSAUTOIR
"DARK DESTROYER"

BORN NOVEMBER 18, 1981 IN ABIDJAN, IVORY COAST.

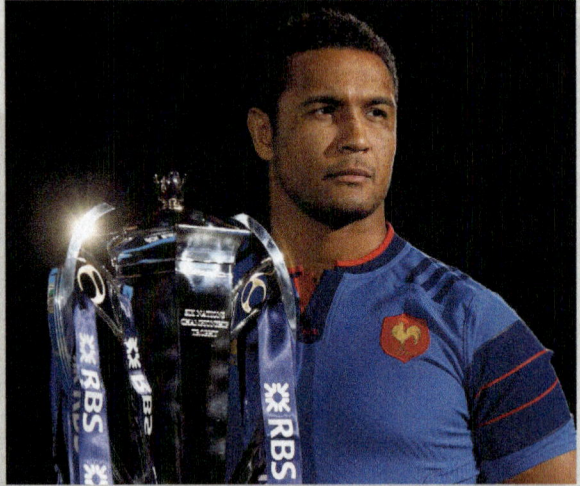

Thierry Dusautoir is famous for his incredible defensive work, his quiet but effective leadership, and his ability to make a large number of tackles in every game. His record 38 tackles in a single match at the 2007 World Cup against New Zealand are remembered fondly.

THE INDOMITABLE WARRIOR OF FRENCH RUGBY

Thierry Dusautoir is famous for his incredible defensive work, his quiet but effective leadership, and his ability to make a large number of tackles in every game. His record 38 tackles in a single match at the 2007 World Cup against New Zealand are remembered fondly. He was recognized for his physical strength, his tackling technique, and his work ethic, making him an essential part of the French team and his club.

Dusautoir left his mark on history with his consistency and his ability to lead by example. His performance at the 2011 World Cup, leading France to within a whisker of the title, is particularly memorable. Off the field, his exemplary behavior and professionalism have made him a respected figure and a role model for young players. He continues to inspire with his integrity and commitment to rugby.

On an individual level, he was voted best player in the world for 2011 by the International Rugby Board and was inducted into the World Rugby Hall of Fame in 2023.

VICTOR MATFIELD, "BIG VIC"

BORN MAY 11, 1977 IN PIETERSBURG, SOUTH AFRICA.

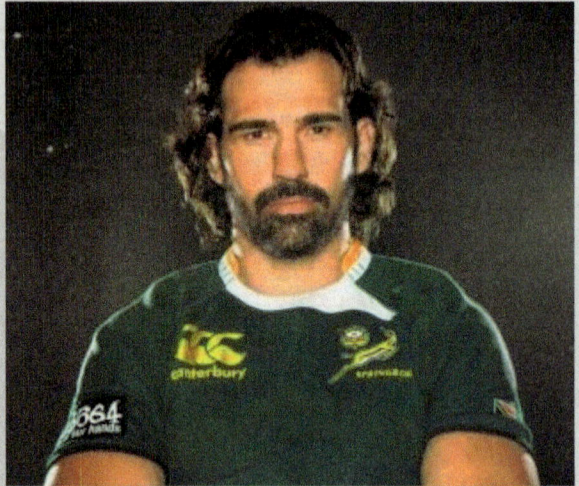

His impressive international career includes winning the 2007 Rugby World Cup with the South African national team. Victor Matfield also won numerous Tri-Nations and Super Rugby championships with the Bulls. Matfield holds the record for South African national team caps for a second row.

THE MASTER OF THE AIR

Victor Matfield is famous for his incredible ability to dominate lineouts, his leadership on the field, and his physical presence. His size and strength allowed him to dominate in the air, but it was his tactical intelligence and ability to read the game that set him apart. He was not only an excellent ball taker but also a leader of men, often responsible for the sideline strategy for his team.

As well as his numerous victories with the Springboks, Matfield was a key part of the Bulls' success in Super Rugby, helping the club to several titles. His retirement, followed by a remarkable comeback for the 2015 World Cup, is a testament to his commitment to the sport and his level of excellence. After his final retirement, he pursued a career as a coach and commentator, sharing his expertise and love of the game.

However, with 108 caps, Matfield is the most capped second row in Springbok history.

US DU RANDT, "US"

Os du Randt is considered one of the best props in rugby history. He is one of the rare players to have won the Rugby World Cup twice, in 1995 and 2007, with the South African national team.

THE ROCK OF THE MELEE

Os du Randt is famous for his physical power, melee technique, and ability to resist opposing forces while supporting his own pack. His longevity in such a demanding position is a testament to his dedication to the game and his professionalism. He was respected by his opponents and admired by his teammates for his quiet strength and unwavering commitment.

Os du Randt left an indelible legacy in rugby, not only for being an integral part of two World Cup-winning teams but also for his continued contribution to the sport in South Africa. His ability to come back from injuries and maintain a high level of performance throughout his career is a testament to his strength of character and talent.

In 2009, he joined the staff of the Free State Cheetahs, with whom he spent part of his club career, as specific scrum coach.

NELSON MANDELA, "MADIBA"

BORN JULY 18, 1918
IN MVEZO,
EASTERN CAPE
PROVINCE, SOUTH
AFRICA.

Nelson Mandela is an emblematic figure of the fight against apartheid in South Africa. His fierce fight for freedom and justice led to his being imprisoned for 27 years by the segregationist apartheid regime. However, he never abandoned his beliefs and continued to fight for a better future for all South Africans.

THE FATHER OF THE RAINBOW NATION AND SYMBOL OF SOUTH AFRICAN RECONCILIATION

Rugby played an important symbolic role in its history. During the 1995 Rugby World Cup, held in South Africa, Nelson Mandela used sport to promote national unity. By wearing the South African national team jersey and supporting the Springboks, Mandela helped bring people together.

During the final of the 1995 Rugby World Cup, organized in South Africa, an emblematic anecdote featured Nelson Mandela. Before the match between the Springboks and New Zealand, Mandela made the surprising decision to wear the South African team's jersey, sporting the number 6, which was that of captain François Pienaar.

Mandela's gesture was a powerful symbol of support for the national team, which was widely seen as representing the reconciliation of the South African nation. During this historic day, the Johannesburg stadium vibrated with shouts of "Madiba" as he presented the World Cup trophy to François Pienaar, thus sealing an unprecedented moment of brotherhood and national unity.

Nelson Mandela, despite his notoriety, was known for his humility and sense of humor. He liked to joke with his security guards and called them his "guardian angels."

26

JOOST VAN DER WESTHUIZEN

BORN FEBRUARY 20, 1971 IN PRETORIA, SOUTH AFRICA

Joost van der Westhuizen was a crucial part of the South African team that won the 1995 World Cup, a landmark in the country's sporting history. During his career he racked up 89 caps for the Springboks and scored 38 tries, a record for a scrum-half at the time.

A LEADER ON AND OFF THE FIELD

Van der Westhuizen is famous for his dynamic play, physical strength and ability to lead his team under pressure. He was known for his ability to break down opposing lines, his tenacious defense and his imposing presence on the pitch. His leadership and determination were key factors in the South African team's success, particularly at the 1995 World Cup.

Besides his sporting achievements, van der Westhuizen is also admired for his strength of character in his fight against Charcot disease, a degenerative condition. After being diagnosed, he dedicated much of his time to raising awareness and funds for neurodegenerative disease research. His courageous public battle against the disease inspired millions of people around the world.

In July 2011, doctors diagnosed Charcot disease, an incurable neurodegenerative condition causing progressive paralysis, difficulty breathing and speaking usually leading to death within 2 to 5 years after diagnosis.

ZINZAN BROOKE, "ZINNY"

BORN FEBRUARY 14, 1965 IN WAIUKU, NEW ZEALAND.

Zinzan Brooke played 58 tests for the All Blacks, including two World Cups, and was a key member of the victorious 1987 World Cup team. Brooke was known for his versatility, his try-scoring ability, and his unusual talent for a forward to score drops, including a famous 48-yard drop at the 1995 World Cup.

BEFORE VISIONARY AND VERSATILE

Zinzan Brooke is famous for his innovative and dynamic style of play, which has often defied stereotypes of his position. He possessed a rare combination of agility, technique and physical strength, which allowed him to contribute in all aspects of the game. His offensive flair, excellent vision of the game and ability to execute decisive actions made him a legend rugby.

Beyond his impact on the field, Brooke is credited with redefining the role of third line center, combining the traditional roles of support and brute force with an ability to actively participate in the offense. His performances in big matches, notably his spectacular drops and daring tries, made rugby history. After his retirement he continued to influence the game as a coach and commentator.

Considered one of the emblematic players of the New Zealand team of the 1990s, he is the older brother of Robin, who was also a New Zealand international, and the younger brother of Martin.

GRANT FOX,"ZORRO"

Grant Fox was a crucial part of the All Blacks team that won the inaugural Rugby World Cup in 1987. During his international career, Fox accumulated an impressive points tally, often topping the points charts in competitions international.

THE FOOT MAESTRO

Fox is famous for his extraordinary ability to score points, whether through penalty kicks, conversions or drops. His precision and consistency have often been decisive in the fate of matches. He was also recognized for his tactical understanding of the game and his ability to direct the attack, making him much more than just a goalscorer.

Grant Fox played a major role in establishing New Zealand as a dominant force in world rugby. Particularly noted was his impact at the 1987 World Cup, where he was the tournament's leading points scorer. Even after his retirement, Fox's legacy lives on, with many scorers drawing inspiration from his technique and mentality.

From 2012 to 2022, he was an independent coach for the New Zealand rugby union team. His role consists of viewing and analyzing All Blacks matches (selection and club) to provide the real coach with his results on the game or the performances of the players.

SHANE WILLIAMS

BORN FEBRUARY 26, 1977 IN MORRISTON, SWANSEA, WALES

Shane Williams holds the Welsh national team record for tries scored, with an impressive total that also places him among the top scorers in international rugby history. He was a key player in the Six Nations Tournament, including the Grand Slams in 2005 and 2008.

THE LIGHTNING WINGER OF WALES

Shane Williams is famous for his blazing speed, agility, and ability to evade defenders much taller than him. Despite his small size for a rugby player, he demonstrated that with enough talent and determination, one can compete at the highest level. His style of play was characterized by daring runs, quick changes of direction, and an ability to create opportunities out of nowhere.

His performances for Wales and the British & Irish Lions made him a fan favorite and rugby legend. Williams was praised for his role in Wales' memorable victories and for his exemplary fair play. After his retirement he continued to be involved in rugby, bringing his passion and experience as a coach and commentator.

Shane Williams was voted World Player of the Year in 2008, becoming the first Welshman to receive this prestigious accolade.

WILLIE JOHN MCBRIDE

Willie John McBride played 63 Tests for Ireland and went on a record five Lions tours. His international career, spanning 13 years, is testament to his durability and influence as a second row. He was also a key member of the Lions team that achieved the famous unbeaten run in South Africa in 1974.

THE INDOMITABLE SOUL OF LIONS

Willie John is famous for his leadership, his physical strength, and his ability to inspire his teammates. He was respected for his toughness, touch play and work ethic. McBride was the prototype of the classic second line, combining strength and intelligence. His leadership during the Lions' unbeaten tour of 1974, where he captained, is particularly noted, cementing his reputation as one of rugby's greatest captains.

Beyond his achievements on the field, McBride left a lasting legacy in rugby, including as a symbol of the Lions spirit. His approach to the game, based on mutual respect and solidarity, continues to influence future generations. After his retirement he continued to serve rugby in various roles, including as manager of the Lions team.

His father, also named William James, died when he was four years old. Her mother raised a family alone, also made up of an eldest daughter and three other boys.

31

MORNÉ DU PLESSIS, "MORNE"

BORN OCTOBER 21, 1949 IN BETHLEHEM, SOUTH AFRICA.

Morné du Plessis was captain of the Springboks and represented South Africa in numerous international tests during the 1970s. He is particularly known for his role as captain during the series against the All Blacks in 1976, where the Springboks won been victorious.

THE SPRINGBOK STANDARD

Morné du Plessis was famous for his playing intelligence, physical strength and leadership qualities. He had a remarkable ability to motivate his teammates and implement winning strategies on the field. His imposing presence and total commitment to his team and his country made him one of the most respected captains.

His career was marked by significant moments, including winning as captain against the All Blacks, one of the most formidable teams of the era. After his retirement, he continued to influence the world of rugby, notably as manager of the South African team which won the World Cup in 1995.

Although from the University of Stellenbosch, the cradle of Afrikaner conservatism, he is a liberal opposed to the policy of apartheid5. He is still one of the important figures in South African rugby.

32

JASON ROBINSON, "BILLY WHIZZ"

BORN JULY 30, 1974 IN LEEDS, ENGLAND

ason Robinson played a key role in the England team that won the Rugby World Cup in 2003. Robinson also shone at club level, notably with Sale Sharks, winning the domestic championship and the European Challenge Cup. He is one of the few players to have reached the pinnacle of rugby union before switching to rugby union.

THE ENGLISH LIGHTNING, MASTER OF ESCAPE

Jason Robinson is famous for his speed, his lightning acceleration and his ability to beat defenders with disconcerting ease. His successful transition from rugby league to rugby union demonstrated his versatility and exceptional talent. His try in the 2003 World Cup final remains one of the most iconic moments of his career, testament to his impact on the game at an international level.

Robinson has been hailed for his significant contribution to both rugby union and rugby union, influencing generations of players in both codes. His electrifying style of play, humble personality and professionalism are often cited as examples to follow. Even after his retirement, he remains an iconic figure in world rugby and a source of inspiration for many young players.

His eldest son, Lewis Tierney, is a rugby league player who notably won the Super League in 2016 with the Wigan Warriors.

33

JONNY SEXTON, "JONNO"

BORN THE
JULY 11, 1985 IN
DUBLIN, IRELAND

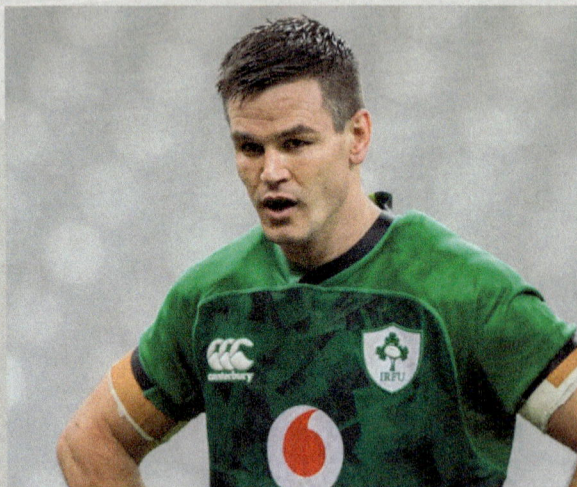

Jonny Sexton played a crucial role in the Irish national team, contributing to several victories in the Six Nations Tournament, including Grand Slams. At club level, he was a central part of Leinster's European Cup successes. Sexton was also named World Rugby Player of the Year in 2018.

THE ARCHITECT OF THE IRISH TRIUMPH

Sexton is famous for his ability to run the offense and make crucial decisions under pressure. His game management, ability to execute complex tactics and resilience are highly valued. He is known for his ability to score points in critical moments, whether through drops, penalties or conversions. His determination and commitment to excellence make him one of the best openers in the world.

Sexton was at the heart of many memorable moments for both Ireland and Leinster, making history with his key performances in decisive matches. His contribution to Irish and European rugby has been immense, raising the level of competition and inspiring future generations of players. His passion for the game and constant desire for improvement continues to distinguish him as a leader on the field.

On September 16 against Tonga, Jonathan Sexton reached 1,090 points scored with the national team, thus breaking the record for the number of points scored by an Irish player, previously held by Ronan O'Gara (1,083 points).

34

KEITH WOOD, "ONCLE FESTER"

BORN JANUARY 27, 1972 IN LIMERICK, IRELAND

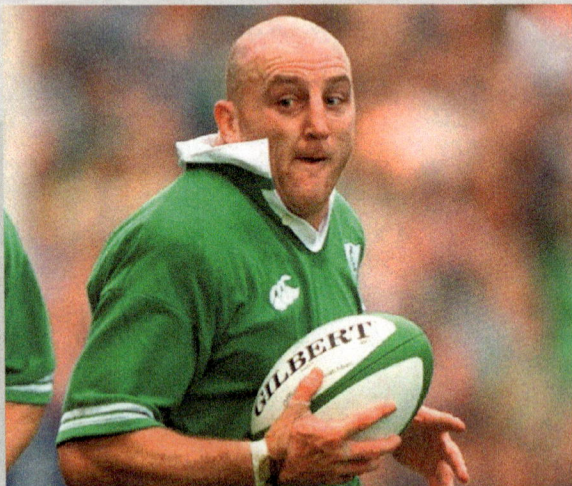

Keith Wood accumulated 58 caps for Ireland and captained the national team. Wood also played for the British and Irish Lions. He is famous for being named IRB Player of the Year in 2001, a rare honor for a forward. At club level, he had a notable career with Harlequins in England.

THE REVOLUTIONARY HOOKER

Keith Wood is famous for redefining the hooker role, bringing an intensity, mobility and technical ability that was uncommon for frontline players at the time. His ability to run with the ball, break the opposition lines, and his incredible work in scrum and touchline set him apart. Wood was also known for his passionate leadership and total commitment to the field.

Highlights of his career include his remarkable performances on the British and Irish Lions tours, as well as his inspirational matches for Ireland in the Six Nations. His passion and style of play has inspired many young players to approach rugby in a more dynamic and involved way, particularly in traditionally more physical roles.

He is the top try scorer among the hookers with 15 goals, ahead of Sean Fitzpatrick and his 13 tries.

35

BRIAN LIMA, "THE CHIROPRACTOR"

BORN JANUARY 25, 1972 IN APIA, SAMOA

Brian Lima is one of the most famous players in Samoan rugby, having played in five Rugby World Cups from 1991 to 2007, a remarkable achievement. Although he did not win major international titles, his longevity, resilience and impressive performances on the field made him a respected and admired player.

THE SAMOAN DESTROYER WITH A HEART OF STEEL

Brian Lima is famous for his fierce tackles and intimidating presence on the field. He has gained a reputation for his precise and powerful defensive interventions, often stopping opposing attacks in their tracks. His ability to inspire his teammates with his tenacity and commitment to the game is also notable. Despite being a tough player on the field, he was respected for his fair play and sportsmanship.

Lima left a lasting mark on rugby, not only for Samoa but also for world rugby. His presence in five Rugby World Cups is a testament to his exceptional talent and determination. He inspired many Samoan and international players with his longevity and passion for rugby. Even after his retirement, his legacy endures as an example of dedication and performance at the highest level.

Brian Lima is the first player to appear in five consecutive World Cups, demonstrating his longevity and passion for rugby.

36

AGUSTÍN PICHOT, "EL PUMA"

BORN AUGUST 22, 1974 IN BUENOS AIRES, ARGENTINA

Agustín Pichot captained the Argentina national team for several years, including their impressive campaign at the 2007 Rugby World Cup where Argentina finished third. He also had a successful club career, notably in Europe with teams like Stade Français.

THE MASTER OF THE ARGENTINA GAME

Agustín Pichot is famous for his passionate leadership, determination and playing intelligence as a scrum-half. His ability to motivate his teammates and lead by example on the field has been a key factor in Argentina's success on the international stage. He was known for his fast play, his tactical vision, and his unfailing commitment.

Argentina's performance in the 2007 World Cup under his captaincy marked a turning point for Argentine rugby, establishing them as a major force in world rugby. His leadership and vision have also been crucial in the advancements of rugby in Argentina, including their inclusion in the Rugby Championship. After his retirement, Pichot continued to influence the world of rugby as an administrator and served as vice-president of World Rugby.

After his career, he became a member of the Argentine Rugby Union Federation in 2009. He worked in particular for Argentina's entry into the Tri-Nations in 2012, and an Argentinian franchise in Super Rugby in 2016.

37

GAVIN HASTINGS, "BIG GAV"

BORN JANUARY 3, 1962 IN EDINBURGH, SCOTLAND

Gavin Hastings has captained the Scottish national team and the British and Irish Lions. During his career he racked up an impressive number of points for Scotland, becoming one of the greatest scorers in rugby history. He also played a crucial role during the Five Nations Tournament and the Rugby World Cup.

THE SHINING STAR OF SCOTTISH RUGBY

Gavin Hastings is famous for his precision with his feet, his solidity in defense and his ability to lead from the back. He was renowned for his long kicks, both in terms of penalties and clearances, as well as his ability to counter-attack with force. His imposing presence and reliability under pressure made him a respected and feared player on the pitch.

His performances for Scotland and the British and Irish Lions were punctuated by many memorable moments, including significant victories in the Five Nations Tournament and inspired performances at the World Cup. His ability to inspire his teammates and convert opportunities into points has often been the key to success for his team. After his retirement he continued to be involved in rugby, contributing to the promotion and development of the sport.

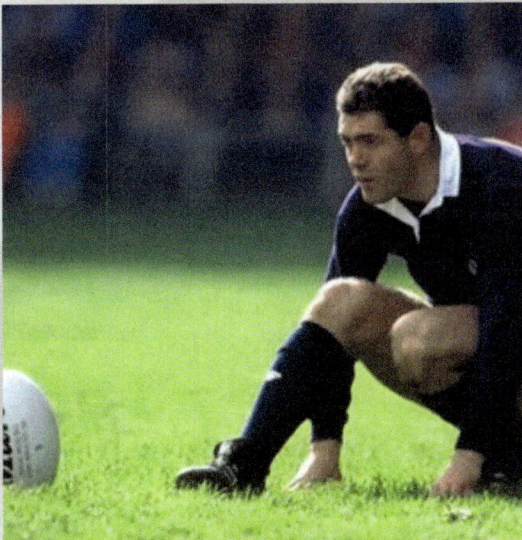

He has ten caps with the Barbarians. He played with Watsonians RFC throughout his career, from 1980 (18 years) to 1997 (35 years) and was their absolute best scorer with 1,203 points scored.

38

JOHN SMIT, "SMITTY"

BORN APRIL 3, 1978 IN PIETERSBURG, SOUTH AFRICA.

John Smit is one of the most iconic captains of the South African national rugby team, the Springboks. He led his team to victory at the 2007 Rugby World Cup. In total, he accumulated 111 caps as a Springbok, making him one of the most capped players in the history of South Rugby. African.

THE STEEL CAPTAIN

John Smit is famous for his exceptional leadership, his ability to unite his team and lead them to victory in critical moments. His exemplary conduct on and off the field inspired his teammates and earned the respect of opponents and fans around the world. His reassuring presence and tactical intelligence were major assets for the Springboks.

The victory in the 2007 World Cup remains the most emblematic moment of his career, crowning a period of success and high competition. His ability to lead a diverse and talented team to victory in such a prestigious tournament is a testament to his caliber as a leader. Smit has also been recognized for his work off the field, including in charity work and rugby development initiatives.

South Africa's player with the most caps as captain, 64 caps, which was once the world record.

39

LAWRENCE DALLAGLIO, "LOL"

BORN AUGUST 10, 1972 IN SHEPHERD'S BUSH, LONDON, ENGLAND

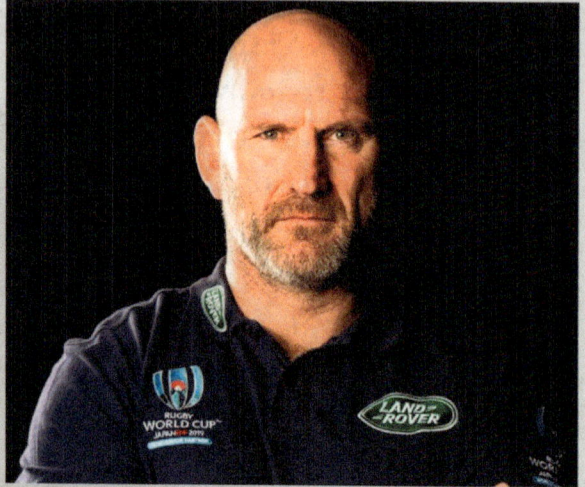

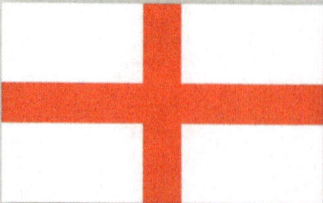

Lawrence Dallaglio was a key member of the England team that won the Rugby World Cup in 2003. Additionally, he enjoyed immense success with his club Wasps, winning multiple Premiership and World Cup titles. European Cup. Dallaglio has 85 caps for England and has captained the national team.

THE UNDISPUTED WARRIOR OF ENGLISH RUGBY

Dallaglio is famous for his physical strength, his versatility on the third line, and his unwavering leadership. He was known for his ability to advance with the ball, his tenacious defense, and his influence both on and off the field. His motivating presence and his unwavering commitment to his team and his country have made him an iconic and respected player.

Dallaglio's career has been punctuated by many highlights, but his part in winning the 2003 World Cup remains his greatest achievement. At club level, he was a pillar of Wasps, contributing to their dominance in English and European rugby for several years. His retirement in 2008 marked the end of an era, but his legacy lives on through his continued contributions to the sport as a commentator and philanthropist.

Loyal throughout his career at London Wasps, Lawrence Dallaglio won at least once all the competitions in which he participated with the English club.

40

JOHN KIRWAN, "JK"

BORN DECEMBER 16, 1964 IN AUCKLAND, NEW ZEALAND

John Kirwan was a key member of the All Blacks during the 1980s and 1990s, playing at the 1987 Rugby World Cup and contributing to New Zealand's victory. During his international career, he scored 35 tries in 63 tests, distinguishing himself for his speed, power and try-scoring ability.

BLACK LIGHTNING OF THE ALL BLACKS

John Kirwan is famous for his incredible speed, strength and ability to break through the defensive line. He scored one of the most memorable tries in World Cup history against Italy in 1987, where he went all the way across the field. His direct and powerful style of play transformed the way the winger was perceived and played.

As well as his on-field performances, Kirwan has been recognized for his work outside of rugby, including raising awareness of mental health. After his retirement, he was openly vocal about his own struggles with depression, becoming an advocate for mental health in sports and beyond. He also went on to have a successful career as a coach.

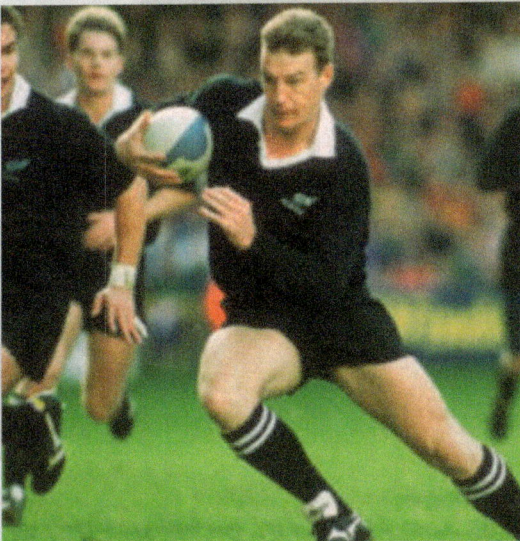

At 1.92 m and 92 kg, he has an enormous size for a winger in the 1980s. At that time, few three-quarters exceeded 80 kg. Built like a third line, he is very powerful and incredibly fast, making him elusive for his opponents.

41

MATT DAWSON, "DAWS"

BORN OCTOBER 31, 1972 IN BIRKENHEAD, ENGLAND

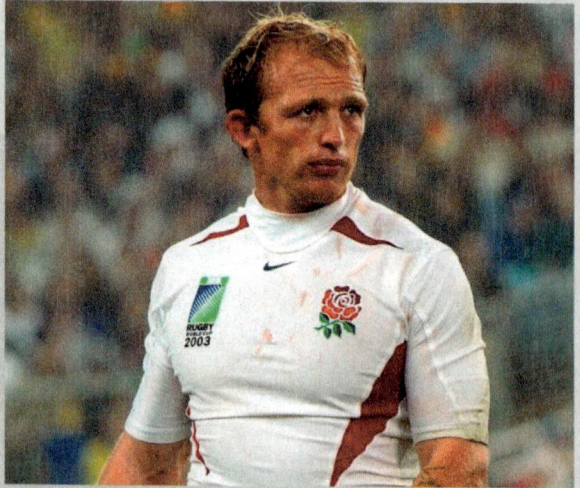

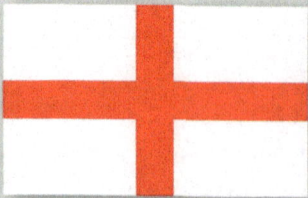

Matt Dawson played the majority of his career for Northampton Saints, where he won several English Premiership and European Cup titles. At international level, Dawson was a key member of the England team during their historic Rugby World Cup victory in 2003.

ENGLAND'S WINNING STRATEGIST

Matt Dawson is famous for his playing intelligence, his liveliness and his ability to implement winning strategies on the field. His fast play and decisions under pressure often changed the course of matches. He was also known for his tenacious defense and his ability to link play between the forwards and the backs.

His performance during the 2003 Rugby World Cup, notably in the final against Australia, was a highlight of his career. His speedy scrumhalf was crucial in keeping the team moving and creating opportunities. Following his retirement from international rugby, Dawson continued to be involved in the sport as a commentator and analyst, sharing his expertise and love for the game.

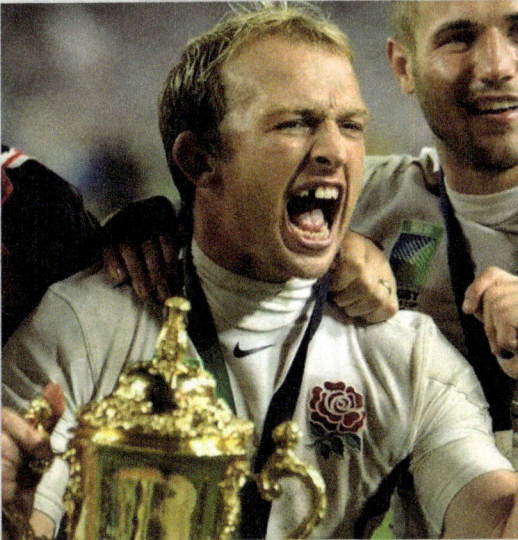

Between 1995 and 2006, Matt Dawson played 77 matches with the England team during which he scored 101 points (16 tries, 6 conversions and 3 penalties).

42

OLLIE CAMPBELL

BORN MARCH 5, 1954 IN DUBLIN, IRELAND

Ollie Campbell was a key part of the Irish national team in the 1970s and 1980s, playing in numerous Five Nations Tournaments. Campbell was particularly renowned for his accuracy as a scorer, racking up an impressive number of points for his national team.

IRELAND'S GOLDEN FOOT MAESTRO

Ollie Campbell is famous for his calmness under pressure and his extraordinary kicking skill. Whether it was conversions, penalties or drops, he was a master of the kicking game, often dictating the pace of the match and racking up crucial points for his team. His ability to manage the game and make strategic decisions has made him an exceptional flyhalf.

Among his many achievements, his performance in the Five Nations Tournament and his contributions during international matches remain notable moments of his career. His elegance on the pitch and his leadership influenced a generation of Irish and international players. After his retirement, Campbell continued to be involved in rugby, bringing his expertise and experience to new generations.

In February 1984, he scored all of Ireland's points, 21 points, against Scotland to win the Triple Crown for the first time since 1948.

43

TONY O'REILLY

BORN MAY 7, 1936
IN DUBLIN,
IRELAND

Tony O'Reilly is one of Irish rugby's most iconic players, having had a distinguished career for both club and national team. Although major titles eluded Ireland during his playing days, O'Reilly was recognized for his exceptional talent as a winger.

THE LEGENDARY WINGMAN

Tony O'Reilly is famous for his speed, his ability to dodge defenders and his impeccable finishing. He was known for his ability to create and convert opportunities, often in critical situations. His physical stature and speed made him a formidable opponent and a spectacular player to watch.

Beyond his performances on the field, O'Reilly is also recognized for his successful career outside of rugby, having achieved success in business and media. His ability to excel in several areas has made him a role model for many athletes aspiring to a career after sport.

Having become a businessman, he held the position of general manager (CEO) then chairman of Heinz from 1987 to 1998.

44

GARETH THOMAS, "ALFIE"

BORN JULY 25, 1974 IN BRIDGEND, WALES

Gareth Thomas is one of Wales' most capped players, having represented his country on several occasions as well as the British and Irish Lions. He was a key player for Wales, participating in several Rugby World Cups and playing a central role in Wales' Grand Slam campaign in the Six Nations.

THE ICONIC WELSH CAPTAIN AND LION OF THE FIELD

Gareth Thomas is famous not only for his exceptional sporting performances but also for his personal courage. He was one of the first rugby players to openly declare his homosexuality, becoming a model of courage and integrity both in the world of sport and in society at large. Her openness and honesty opened an important dialogue about acceptance and inclusion in sport.

In addition to his accomplishments on the field, Thomas' influence extends far beyond through his commitment to diversity and inclusion. He has worked actively to combat homophobia in sport and to support people in similar situations. His work has been widely recognized and he continues to inspire many people around the world.

In 2006, he received the Pat Marshall Award from the British specialist press (within the Rugby Union Writers Club, created in 1961), for having been named best European player for the year 2005.

45

FELIPE CONTEPOMI

BORN AUGUST 20, 1977 IN BUENOS AIRES, ARGENTINA

Felipe Contepomi has racked up an impressive number of caps for the Pumas, appearing at several Rugby World Cups and often being his team's main points scorer. At club level, he enjoyed notable success in Europe, notably with Leinster in Ireland, where he won the European Cup.

FELIPE CONTEPOMI, A MAESTRO OF THE GAME

Felipe Contepomi is famous for his offensive play, his ability to direct the game, and his exceptional precision with his foot. He was a master tactician, known for his vision of the game and his ability to inspire his teammates. His competitiveness and passionate commitment on the field made him a fan favorite and a feared opponent.

Contepomi has been a key player in Argentina's rise on the international stage, most notably at the 2007 Rugby World Cup where Argentina finished third. His leadership and performances helped raise the status of rugby in Argentina and inspire a new generation of players. Off the field, he is also recognized for his career in medicine, having continued his studies and practice alongside his rugby career.

Having become backline coach of the Argentina team in 2022 under the direction of Michael Cheika, Felipe Contepomi succeeds him as coach of the Pumas in December 2023.

46

SIR WILSON WHINERAY
"THE BIG BEAR"

BORN JULY 10, 1935 IN AUCKLAND, NEW ZEALAND

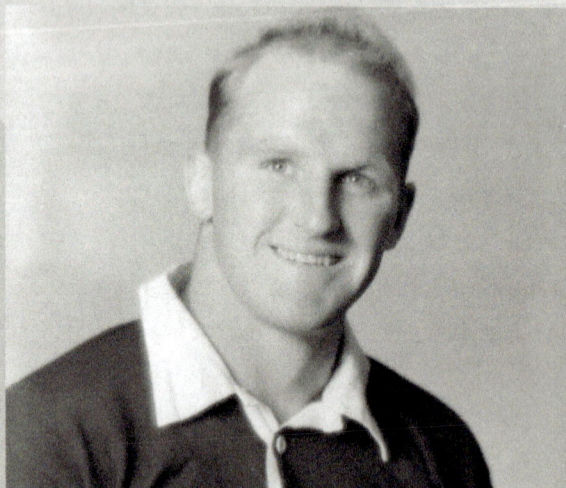

During his career, Sir Wilson Whineray led the All Blacks in numerous international tests, gaining worldwide respect for his leadership and performance. He captained the All Blacks more than 30 times and was recognized for his fair play, sportsmanship and respect for his opponents.

THE GIANT BEAR WHO SHAPED ALL BLACKS HISTORY

Sir Wilson Whineray is famous for his exceptional leadership, scrum strength and ability to motivate his teammates. He embodied the spirit of rugby, with a commitment to excellence and an ability to lead his team through significant challenges. His name remains synonymous with dedication, respect and success in the world of rugby.

Whineray was a role model for many players and was involved in rugby well after his retirement as a player. He was inducted into the World Rugby Hall of Fame, and his contribution to the sport was recognized beyond the field with a knighthood for his services to rugby and the community.

Whineray was inducted into the Rugby Hall of Fame in 1999 for his outstanding contributions to the sport and culture of rugby.

47

BOBBY SKINSTAD

BORN JULY 3, 1976 IN BULAWAYO, ZIMBABWE

Bobby Skinstad was a key player for the South African national team, the Springboks, during the 1990s and early 2000s. He was recognized for his versatility as a flanker, capable of playing both in number 6, 7 and 8 with great efficiency.

THE SOUTH AFRICAN ACE WHO CONQUERED THE RUGBY WORLD

Bobby Skinstad is famous for his charisma and leadership on the field. He had an undeniable presence, capable of motivating his teammates and changing the course of the game. His athleticism, combined with his ability to read the game and make strategic decisions, made him one of the most dynamic players in the game. its time.

During his career, Skinstad has had several notable moments, including his appearances in World Cups and his performances in Super Rugby. Following his retirement from professional rugby, he remained involved in the sport as a commentator and analyst, bringing his expertise and passion for rugby to a wider audience.

Some accuse Skinstad of shying away from the dark work of conquest specific to the role before and of only seeking to "hunt" the attempt.

48

GERALD DAVIES, "THE GHOST"

BORN FEBRUARY 7, 1945 IN LLANSAINT, WALES

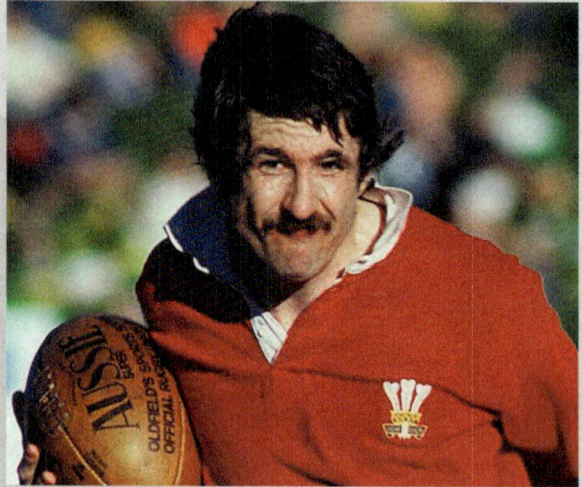

With a distinguished international career, Gerald Davies was a key member of the Welsh team during the 1960s and 1970s, a golden era for Welsh rugby. He featured on several British and Irish Lions tours and was a central part of Wales' Grand Slam campaigns in the Five Nations.

THE GHOST, THE WELSH LIGHTNING OF RUGBY

Gerald Davies is famous for his elegant playing style, speed and incredibly smooth movements. He was known for his ability to avoid tackles and outwit the opposing defense with exceptional grace and agility. His ability to create tries out of nothing was legendary, and he was often a gem in the Welsh attack.

Beyond his performances on the pitch, Davies is recognized for his fair play and exemplary behavior. He left an indelible mark on Welsh rugby and is often cited among the best players of his era. After retiring from sport, he pursued a successful career in journalism and was involved in rugby administration, contributing to the sport's legacy long after hanging up his boots.

Gerald Davies was appointed manager during the 2009 British Lions tour to South Africa.

MARK ANDREWS, "BIG EASY"

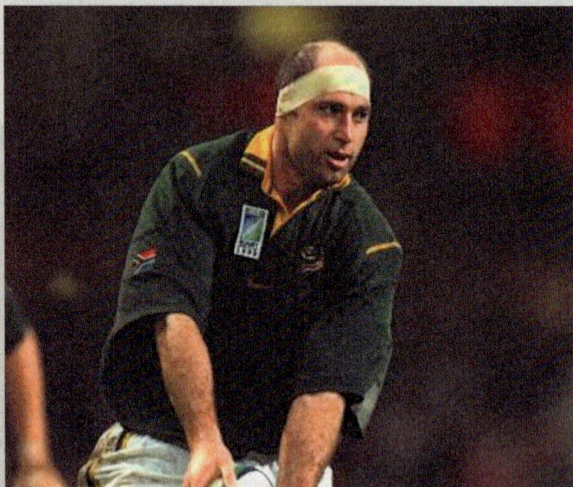

Mark Andrews was a crucial member of the Springbok team that won the Rugby World Cup in 1995, a historic moment not only for South African rugby but also for the nation as a symbol of post-war unity. apartheid. Andrews also enjoyed a successful club career, including playing for the Sharks in Super Rugby.

THE PILLAR OF SOUTH AFRICAN VICTORIES

Mark Andrews is famous for his versatility on the pitch, capable of playing in both the second and third lines. His size, strength and touch skills have made him a key player on any team. His playing intelligence and ability to execute complex strategies have been major assets for the Springboks and his club teams.

His participation in the 1995 World Cup remains the highlight of his career, symbolizing hope and reconciliation for South Africa through sport. He continued to play an important role for the Springboks and his club, showing a consistency and performance that elevated him among the greats of South African rugby.

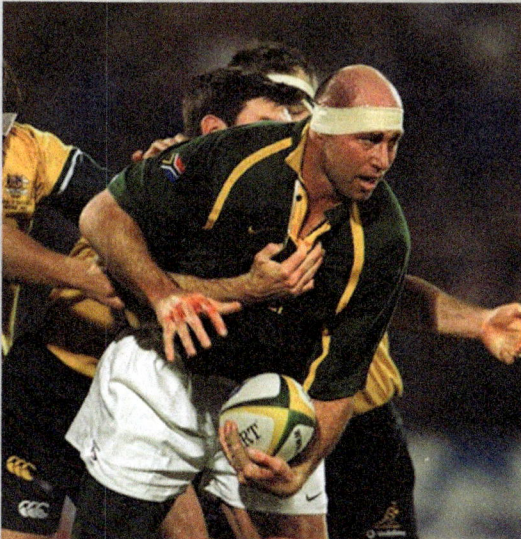

After his retirement he became manager of a brand management company in Durban and owns two breeding farms.

BILL BEAUMONT

Bill Beaumont captained England and led his team to numerous successes in the Five Nations Tournament, including a Grand Slam in 1980. He was also a prominent member of the British and Irish Lions. After retiring from sport, Beaumont had a notable career as a rugby manager.

A CHARISMATIC LEGEND OF ENGLISH RUGBY

Bill Beaumont is famous for his natural leadership, fair play and game intelligence. He was renowned for his ability to inspire his teammates and maintain strong cohesion and discipline within his team. His impact on the field was complemented by his commitment and integrity off the field.

In addition to his achievements as a player, Beaumont had a considerable influence on rugby as an administrator, working to promote the sport and strengthen its integrity and accessibility. His dedication to both the competitive aspect and governance of rugby has made him a respected figure well beyond his playing career.

He joined the International Rugby Hall of Fame in 20039. He was appointed Commander of the Order of the British Empire in 2008 for services to English rugby and charity.

It is with deep emotion that we close this extraordinary journey through the 50 legends of rugby and their history. As we close this book, we are filled with gratitude to these rugby heroes who have captured our hearts and inspired us with their talent and devotion to the game.

Every page of this book is a celebration of the spirit of camaraderie, fair play and passion that makes rugby more than just a sport, but a way of life. The stories of these legendary players are a powerful reminder of the importance of teamwork, surpassing oneself and perseverance to achieve excellence.

We would like to thank each of these players for their invaluable contribution to rugby and global sporting culture. Their legacy will live on through future generations, continuing to inspire young talents to dream big and embrace the values of rugby.

We hope that this book has made you feel the very essence of rugby, a sport that transcends borders and unites people around a common passion. May the spirit of rugby continue to shine on the pitches, in the stands and in the hearts of all fans.

Printed in Great Britain
by Amazon